a

SPANNER

in the

WORKS

Memoirs of
an East End Girl

EILEEN B. WILTCHER

RETHINK PRESS

First published in Great Britain 2017
by Rethink Press (www.rethinkpress.com)

© Copyright Eileen B. Wiltcher

Contents

Who do you think you are?

Once, people lived their lives, got on with whatever came their way, and asked few questions. What happened behind closed doors stayed behind closed doors.

If one moved in prestigious circles, one might have had 'expectations': expectations brought about through family wealth, position, connections or family history. For the majority, however, it was enough to be concerned with the here and now: earning enough to put food on the table and keeping a roof over one's head.

Then the explosion of new technology pushed us into a world of previously unknown dimensions and transformed ordinary lives. Television sets invaded our living rooms and the rest of the world was suddenly much closer. Local news became global news and global news became local news.

The new millennium ushered in the television series Who Do You Think You Are? What a few dozen cans of worms that programme unleashed! Parish registers led to the discovery of heroes, black sheep, trailblazers, immigrants, emigrants and even a few convicts. How engrossing it was to sit in an armchair and watch the revelations of celebrities laid bare. The programme spawned a relatively new hobby for the masses of establishing a family tree, and suddenly grandparents were put under the microscope. Computers were fired up and search engines became all-invasive. It was exciting stuff – but wait! Curiosity killed the cat, didn't it? Curiosity can prove cruel; curiosity can shine a harsh light where broken dreams lie in the dusty cobwebs and a protective arm can no longer shield a dear one. Times change, the once unacceptable becomes the unremarkable and it seems that money can buy anything, including silence. It wasn't always thus.

One day, my elder daughter posed a casual question about family origins; she was intrigued, and perhaps a little dismayed, by my reply. Hitherto we had been leading our busy lives – giving birth, growing up, forging careers, struggling with a mortgage – and somehow, origins had never cropped up. Suddenly, the past was important. Who did we think we were? What about the old ones? I heard my mother's voice, 'Mind your own business'. But today privacy is almost impossible and indeed, all sorts of business is thrust into the public arena.

So now our story begins, but please be gentle with my dear ones; they haven't asked to be revealed and remember, their world was very different.

A Half Pint on Thursday

The whispering night stretches
its teasing limbs and
behind my sleepless eyes
come old jaunts anew,
a cavalcade of family passes through,
strangely clear like yesterday.

Billy reluctantly opened his eyes to the early grey light of a perishing cold January morning and gradually became aware of familiar noises issuing from downstairs – the rattling of the grate, the raking of cinders and muted cussings as the fire refused to light. Then the coldness of the day enveloped his entire being as he remembered that his mother was dead and it was his older sister Beattie who was downstairs starting up the day for him and his father. His other sisters, Bessie and Florrie, were now married and gone from the family home in Queens Road, and Billy missed them; he missed their kindness, the sound of their voices and their good-natured joshing. Life was bleak. In a spasm of gut-wrenching misery, Billy wished desperately that he could turn back the clock. After a year or more this was still a home and family in mourning.

His sister Beattie called him downstairs for breakfast; his day had begun. As he shrugged on his heavy jacket, he glanced at his sister and thought how tired and pale she looked. There was a quietness about her; no usual jolly word to send him off into his day.

By the time Billy Driscoll got to the end of Queens Road, he knew that something was seriously not right. As he turned up his collar against the bitter wind, a picture of Beattie's poor ashen face struck him afresh. With a sudden sickening sense of rising panic, he spun on his heel and, instead of heading towards the bus for the docks, he hot-footed it straight back for home; by the time number seventeen was in his sights, he was running. Once inside he momentarily leaned against the door, getting his breath back, but even then he was aware of the unusual atmosphere. Moving towards the stairs, he heard the faint mewing of a cat. Stopping outside his sister's bedroom, he put his ear to the door. The mewing became more insistent. He gently pushed open the door and saw his sister on her bed, clutching a tiny scrap of something wrapped in a towel. His sister's eyes opened, fastened on his and she gasped, 'Billy… baby… doctor!' Billy shot out of the house, down the road and into the surgery.

Doctor Brenda arrived at number seventeen just as old Bill was pulling up his braces and wondering why his daughter wasn't at the stove cooking his haddock. Having completed all the midwifery tasks, and now drinking a cup of tea with the two Bills, the doctor pronounced both mother and baby girl well, but she urged them to call her if the new mother became anxious or the four-pound scrap did not feed well. The two bewildered men nodded and looked helplessly at each other. Here was a dilemma, indeed – my arrival had truly thrown a spanner in the works. I was the surprise package that no one had anticipated, least of all my mother!

For the first four weeks of my life I was Eileen Beatrice Driscoll until my father, Walter Octavius Levett the Second, deigned to make an honest woman of my mother. It was a case of in and out of the registry office and home for fish and chips. Not

Aforetimes – Casting Off

One day they left
and journeyed to another land.
So young in years
but hope held out her hand.

When the families of Mary Ann Cornhill from Faversham and Frances Ann Saffery Newman from Sheerness abandoned the gentle balmy air of Kent and made their individual pioneering journeys to the Smoke, they had each hoped to find work, opportunities and good prospects. What they found was fog, soot, belching factory chimneys, friction and fierce rivalries. This was the Isle of Dogs, and Poplar in particular, round about the mid-1800s and for sure, the grimy streets were not paved with gold. There was plenty of other detritus lying about, including many a pile of steaming horse shit, but not a gold sovereign amongst it.

Once arrived, like so many others, clutching their

few belongings and surveying the far-from-pleasant land, there they stayed. The task of survival began – a task shared with the Irish and Jewish immigrants, all vying for work in the street markets, the rag trade, the factories and the docks.

What of prospects? They were few and far between, but both young women in the fullness of time found husbands and produced large families. Mary Ann married Dennis Driscoll in 1850. He was an Irish labourer lately from County Cork. Young Frances Ann was courted by Henry Terry, whom she married in 1866. Both marriages were marked by events that heralded the sign of things to come. Soon after Mary Ann's Christmas Day wedding, a brilliant meteor was seen travelling across the night sky, causing much excitement and many predictions for the future.

During the 1850s Charles Dickens was a popular and prominent writer, and as editor of the journal Household Words gave much space and support to the campaign for improved sanitation and investigations into the root causes of the cholera and typhoid epidemics, which were ravaging London at that time.

Sixteen years later on 12 July, when Frances Ann became Mrs Henry Terry, the Islington Gazette reported there were as many as two hundred and fifty new cases of cholera a week. Eventually, a stringent cleaning recipe was recommended for sinks in dwellings and thankfully, the epidemic in 1866 proved to be the last. In 1870 the first water closets were introduced.

This was the time when Doctor Barnardo walked the streets of East London, grieving the plight of the hungry, destitute children abandoned through death or desertion by their parents. He saw boys sleeping rough on rooftops and dying in alleyways. He set up his Ragged School in the hope that the boys would come to him, and many, though fearful, did. It was better than the dreaded workhouse.

Both the Driscolls and the Terrys eventually produced a bevy of sons and daughters, all hard-working and dutiful, but undoubtedly times were hard and every single penny earned was needed. Those men who were fortunate to be earning regularly might receive a standard wage of between twenty-two and thirty shillings a week; the unskilled received much less. There was plenty of space on the kitchen table for empty plates.

The Terrys and the Driscolls

Hardly Montagues and Capulets
but certainly just as feisty,
the Terrys and the Driscolls
about to be united.

Among the Terry offspring was one Beatrice Frances, and, according to the local likely lads, she was the best-looking girl in Millwall. Beattie was a bubble of laughter, never still, shifting from hope to new hope and gathering up everyone around her. Slim and dark, with eloquent brown eyes, she was indeed a beauty. She was quick to dance and sing, quick to do a good turn, and people easily took to her. But she did not tolerate unkindness and fairly often she could be found at the centre of a street disturbance, when she might have spotted a carter being vicious to his horse or a kid being clouted for picking up a fallen orange from a barrow. Beattie was never short of admirers but gently laughed them off as she went her own independent way. There was always another day for Beattie.

Beattie found herself a place of work at C&E Mortons Canning Factory in Cubitt Town. Here she stood for hour upon grinding hour, working for a pittance. There were, however, a few pleasant distractions, one of which was a football team, its origins at Mortons in about 1858. It gloried in the name of Mill Road Rovers and a local pub was used as the team's headquarters and changing rooms. This team of lads was generally known to the locals as the Sextons, named after the pub landlord, Maurice John Sexton. Later it was renamed Millwall and the club continued to survive the turn of the century and beyond. During Beattie's day, its supporters were loyal, fiercely partisan and very vocal, typifying the East End fighting spirit.

A sinister distraction in 1888, and certainly not a welcome one, was the activity of the murderer of prostitutes, Jack the Ripper. 'A terrible crime has been committed!' was the newspaper seller's cry after the discovery of the first Ripper murder. It struck terror into the hearts of the East Enders and certainly into that of Beattie, who couldn't forget the chilling words as she laid her head on her pillow at night. As the crimes proliferated and journalistic sensationalism took over, there was much speculation about these never-to-be-solved horrendous crimes. Suggestions that the murderer was a surgeon, a maddened gentleman or even a member of the royal family were put forward. It was thought that whoever it might be had more than a passing knowledge of the female anatomy. The reputation of the East End grew ever darker.

Although at the time Beattie's wages were poor and working conditions were grim, she was marginally better treated than some and there had been a slight upturn in wages. However, in truth the labour force was a pool of desperate souls seeking to scrape together a living merely to survive.

No small influence on this state of affairs was the occasion of the momentous Dock Strike of 1889, when the dock workers called a crippling all-out strike and demanded an increase in their hourly rate. They called for a basic rate of sixpence an hour. After six weeks of appalling hardship for the men and their families, who were on the verge of starvation, they won the day and the Millwall Docks were eventually reopened. Thousands of pounds had been sent from sympathetic workers in Australia who had donated their own wages to the cause. At home, the wealthier middle classes had been impressed by the orderliness of the marches and the patient determination of the men to see it through. When Cardinal Manning acted as a sympathetic mediator between the dock owners and the strikers, the Government and the people listened. Colonel G. R. Birt, the general manager at the Millwall Docks, gave evidence to a parliamentary committee by commenting on the awful physical conditions of the workers, who often came to work without boots on their feet and not having eaten for several days. Finally, the tide was turned. The dispute also encouraged the burgeoning of fledgling trade unions and the rumblings of the infant Labour Party. Times were changing; the strike for the dockers' tanner became a true moment of history.

By the beginning of the 1890s Beattie had met and married William Dennis Driscoll and had gone to live temporarily with his family on West Ferry Road. And what a family!

The tiny terraced house groaned at the seams with brothers and sisters, and in charge of them all was Mary Ann, lately of Faversham and now the mother-in-law with no equal. To say she kept a tight ship was the understatement of all time, and Beattie, despite now being a wife, was left in no doubt about who was the guv'nor. Mary Ann had been widowed by Dennis Driscoll, with whom she had produced eight children. They had lived then in a neat terraced house in Mellish Street, Poplar. The mystery was how they had all squeezed into that little house. With two downstairs rooms and a scullery boasting a tin bath on a nail, it was hardly the Ritz but, unbelievably, it was far superior to many others. By 1891 Mary Ann was living in West Ferry Road, having married again and become briefly a Mackenzie, but was now once more a widow. Nonetheless, there was still plenty of fire in her boiler. Bill Driscoll, her hard-working, dutiful son, was always at her beck and call and was sent daily to fetch her jug of porter, her preferred ale.

Boiler-maker Bill Driscoll was a bundle of a man. Only strangers messed with Bill, and they only tried it once. He was of medium height, stocky in stature with arms like pistons; arms that lifted and swung mighty hammers day in, day out. Yet Bill was a gentle man. Good-natured and generous to any good cause, he shared what he had with one exception – his tool bag. His tools were his wealth, his true treasure, and anyone who attempted to help themselves was swiftly sorted. The thief who stole a workman's tools was, according to Bill, the scum of the earth. Bill worked mercilessly hard for his wages and his tools earned him his bread, so woe betide the fingers that lifted so much as a ruler. His shock of auburn curls was never completely subdued by his old cloth cap, and the twinkling blue Irish eyes that looked out on the day never failed to see some humour in the grim surroundings. He walked with a roll and never once doubted his place in the world.

In 1893 Bill realised that the time had come for a change. With his mother still fiercely demanding and his wife now pregnant and increasingly resentful of her mother-in-law, marriage was not providing the home comforts he had anticipated. He and Beattie left West Ferry Road and moved to Hind Street, and here, in May 1894, Beatrice, their first-born, arrived. Mary Ann was hardly overjoyed and, truth be known, she was somewhat jealous; there was no way she was going to take a back seat and watch her beloved Billy give undivided attention to his wife and baby. The baby grew and was bonny and Beattie's delight, but, strangely, she showed little sign of wanting to move. Mary Ann in her spiteful wisdom pronounced curvature of the spine, but she scoffed at the idea of consulting a doctor – in her opinion, an unnecessary indulgence. But one day the baby astounded them all: she stood up and walked around the room. Beattie clasped her hands in joy and looked towards the visiting Mary Ann, who merely sniffed and left the room.

A New Beginning

I'll give you a song
of lives that are gone,
of hearts that were broken in two.
I'll sing you a song of love that was strong
and two hearts for ever true.

With another baby on the way, the family of three moved to Upper North Street and here Elizabeth (to be known as Bessie) was born, a playmate for Beatrice. Theirs was a loving, caring home and Bill was a good provider, but his days in the docks were long and back-breaking. Leaving home in early morning darkness, carrying a heavy bag of tools as he walked to the docks, he was one of many struggling to earn enough to put food on the table and boots on the family's feet. At the end of the day Beattie would often find him asleep, sitting bolt upright at the kitchen table with a fork in his hand and his meal half-eaten. Bill adored his Beattie and despite all the hardship they were happy together.

Beattie was liked in the street; she always managed to find a cheery word for the other mothers and when she heard of extra hardship – an out-of-work father or an illness – somehow she managed to conjure up an extra plate of stew, adding a dumpling or two or even a bit of suet pudding. Sometimes, sworn to secrecy, she would even pass over a few precious coppers so that a mother could redeem her bedsheets or wedding ring from the pawnbrokers – or 'uncles', as they were known. This was a regular practice when wages ran out halfway through the week or had been drunk away at the pub. It was not uncommon to see wives waiting outside a pub on a Friday night, hoping to get some housekeeping money before the rest was swallowed in drink.

Paying the rent was everything. No rent money could mean a family was put out on the street. Accommodation was horrifyingly crowded. There could be three women in a bed and the space under it rented out; if a man did shift work, his bed was rented out to another until he came home. However, it was important to keep up a veneer of respectability and the pawnbrokers thrived. Beattie's neighbour Maudie often 'popped her saucepans', much to her shame, but she had no other option. Her husband was a docker and often out of work. Beattie sometimes met her on the corner to press a few coppers into her hand, remarking on Maudie's latest black eye or swollen cheek. 'It don't mean anyfing Beat, 'e's raging mad at being turned away agin.' 'Turned away' was the fate of many casual labourers who crowded round the dock gates, hoping to be picked for a day's work.

It was a miserable life for many of Beattie and Bill's neighbours. Mothers got on with their lot, somehow surviving the drudgery, the abuse and birth after birth.

At one end of the street lived an old woman they called Mother Knocker-Up. No longer employed, she spent her time in the better weather sitting on the wall outside a shabby house. Hour after hour, wrapped in shawls, with a clay pipe hanging from her lips, she watched the comings and goings. The little kids were scared of her because of the strange tales that were spun about her. In her younger years, she had indeed been a 'knocker-up' – someone who, armed with a pea-shooter and an ample supply of peas, was employed to wake the market traders in the early hours. No one dared be late in those days – unpunctuality cost you your job! No job, no rent, no food, no bed.

The pub was a place of escapism after the harsh realities of the factories and the docks. To be sure, there were street-corner music halls throughout the East End and plenty of bawdy entertainment; young girls gathered up their petticoats and danced to the music of the street barrel organ and families held little gatherings in their tiny front parlours, where they sat round a piano and sang the popular songs of the day. Dan Leno was the most famous comedian of his generation and first appeared in pantomime in 1888. He is reputed to have been the greatest of all the panto dames and is revered in music-hall circles as master of his art. Another great performer, Harry Champion, with his costermonger songs like 'Boiled Beef and Carrots', 'Any Old Iron' and 'I'm Henery the Eighth, I Am' was hugely popular. Of course, any boozy gathering could be reduced to tears by a rendering of the sentimental 'My Old Dutch'. The ladies, never to be outdone, graced the Victorian stage and one such Florrie Forde warbled 'Down at the Old Bull and Bush' and 'Oh! Oh! Antonio'. The

American Ella Shields, who dressed as a somewhat elegant tramp, brought to fame 'Burlington Bertie from Bow'. Last but never least was the incomparable Marie Lloyd, born in Hoxton, who sang her saucy songs to adoring music-hall audiences and brought the house down with 'A Little Of What You Fancy Does You Good'. It is said that her funeral was attended by fifty thousand people. In spite of the harshness of their lives, the East Enders knew how to enjoy themselves and their lively sense of humour was never far away.

At the heart of that melting pot of humanity, amongst the tenements and squalid streets, the Jewish theatre thrived. The tailoring sweatshops, the market traders and the jewellery workers provided audiences who relished the quick and ready wit of their own comedians and their soul-searching music. This was a time when people made their own entertainment. A stroll in the park, a meagre picnic or even a trip on the Thames: all these were truly appreciated.

Now living in Augusta Street, Beattie gave birth to twin boys Billy and Frankie. How sisters Beatrice and Bessie adored them! Exhausted as she was, mother Beattie continued to work the clock round, doing her best to keep the house clean, the children fed and her husband nourished. On Saturday nights, she shopped in bustling Chrisp Street Market, buying the cheaper cuts of meat and a bit of steak for Bill's breakfast. The joint had to last the week, first with the addition of Yorkshire puddings, then turned into stew with dumplings, then a little meat pie with pastry and jugs of gravy, and maybe on Thursday the remainder was padded out with a tiny bit of skirt and some more precious potatoes. Bread and dripping made up the children's tea, with the occasional lump of bread pudding without the fruit. Bread and margarine was the usual fare – on a good day some jam appeared on the table, but that wasn't too often.

The Augusta Street community was by and large a safe neighbourhood but, like anywhere else, it housed its fair share of questionable characters. Despite this, seldom were front doors locked, perhaps because no one had anything worth pinching.

One memorable morning, Beatrice was sitting on the doorstep with a small cone of dolly mixtures in her hand when from nowhere came a violent shove. The cone was knocked flying, the dolly mixtures scattered across the pavement. She shouted and jumped up, and then dived to rescue the sweets from the dirty concrete, but the ragged boy who had pushed her was already on his knees scooping up the sweets and desperately shovelling them into his mouth. Beatrice tried to cover as much as she could with her outstretched hand, but the boy jumped up and brought a vicious boot down on her fingers. She screamed with pain and the boy took off, leaving her to nurse her bloodied hand and broken fingernails. Her nails never grew properly again and one of her fingers was permanently misshapen. Despite poor Beatrice's misfortune, her kindly mother sympathised with the lad and pointed out how dreadful it must be to be so hungry.

Bill watched anxiously over his precious boys whenever he could and Beattie cherished them, but in the year 1900 Frankie, dangerously weakened by bronchitis and the onset of convulsions, closed his eyes on the world. Billy was left, stretching out his hands, constantly seeking his missing brother. There was a terrible bleakness in Augusta Street; the other mothers in the neighbourhood all felt Beattie's grief. Her once beautiful face was set in a mask of sadness.

Then in July 1901, in the midst of a violent thunderstorm, Florence entered centre stage. The rain lashed the windows and the old brass bed knobs were covered in towels to prevent a lightning strike on the bed and its precious contents. Bowls of hot water came and went whilst Bill anxiously stood guard. The birth was tough and Beattie was exhausted,

A Grand Day Out

Daisies and dandelions
buttercups and joy,
a day full of sunshine,
no cloud to destroy
hours full of wonder
for each girl and boy.

Once the days began to edge towards springtime
and after-school evenings were lighter, the girls
escaped the house and, looping their skipping ropes
over the gas lamps in the street, made improvised
swings. Boys careered boisterously up and down
the road in their home-made wooden carts, and
babies were lodged outside front doors to take some
debatable fresh air and watch the noisy goings-on.

Mothers in their aprons who had five minutes to spare stood on their doorsteps and gossiped. The lighter evenings provided a lift in their lives, and those who could do made the most of it.

One morning young Beatrice, the budding pioneer of Augusta Street, gathered up a band of youngsters and led them into an adventure. None of them knew where they were going, least of all Beatrice, but the magic word 'out' had seized their imaginations and the expedition began. Armed with a couple of bottles of water, a few bread-and-marge sandwiches and not a farthing between them, they marched off. The day was theirs and wherever Beatrice led they willingly followed; she was the Pied Piper of Augusta Street. They dallied a while in a nearby scrubby park, picking sooty flowers and gaudy dandelions, but then they were off again, passing along unknown streets and through strange neighbourhoods. Suddenly, they found themselves at close quarters with the formidable River Thames. They gazed in awe at the imposing buildings on the far bank. With a 'Come on, you lot!' Beatrice propelled them into the Greenwich Foot Tunnel. Excitedly, they hopped and skipped their way beneath the river, out into Greenwich and eventually into the unknown leafy expanse of a huge park.

Here was a freedom that made them delirious. Under the watchful eye of Beatrice they rolled down hills, climbed trees and chased birds, shouting and laughing in the spring sunshine until their legs grew tired. They played until the sun began to sink, when Beatrice called time on their enjoyment. The tired but happy children began the journey home, Beatrice carrying the smaller ones in turn.

Meanwhile, back in Augusta Street, a queue of agitated mothers had formed on Beattie's doorstep, all wanting to know the whereabouts of their children. Although young Beatrice's child-minding skills were often called upon up and down the street, the lateness of the hour had brought about a feeling of alarm. Poor besieged Beattie was as baffled and concerned as the other mothers were. Her only response was to assure them that Beatrice hadn't taken them far and that she was sure they would be back soon (silently, she promised her eldest daughter a clip round the ear when she had her over the doorstep).

At last the motley tribe came into sight, as dirty and bedraggled as the dandelions they clutched. Relief soon turned into anger as the mothers rounded up their offspring and dragged them indoors. Beatrice, now left alone, was grabbed by the arm, hauled up the step and frogmarched down the passage. Twisting away from her mother's grip, Beatrice asked, 'What have I done?' Her mother wasted no time in telling her, the words extravagantly coloured to impress upon her the seriousness of the escapade.

Young Beatrice took the flack, secretly thinking to herself, 'So what?' They'd had a corker of a day and all the kids had enjoyed themselves.

It has to be said, however, that as Beattie closed her eyes that night, she smiled in the darkness and acknowledged a little stab of pride. Her daughter had given those little 'uns a good time and brought them all safely home. She really was a bloody marvel. What stories those children told and what treasured memories had been made!

Boiler-Maker Bill

Give me the chance of the job, mister
I will not serve you wrong.
My hammers will sing down the hours, sir
I'll graft the whole day long.
I've sweat to give for the job, sir
you'll find I'm willing and true.
A fair day's pay and respect, sir
that's all I expect from you.

Bill was sometimes sent to work in Pennyfields, an area inhabited by the Chinese community, around whom the East Enders had spun a web of mystery and intrigue. As always, ignorance bred suspicion and tales of 'strange goings-on' and the setting up of opium dens proliferated. Beatrice was occasionally sent to deliver her father's sandwiches or bread pudding, especially if he had gone to work on an empty stomach. She didn't enjoy this task but being the eldest, she had no option. She kept her eyes down and scurried back to Augusta Street as fast as she could.

Beatrice by nature was a contented girl. She was a giggler who was quick to appreciate a comical turn of events, but she was equally quick to spot an injustice, and then her brown eyes would spark with displeasure and she was slow to forgive. In company she stood back, but she was seldom overlooked; her beautiful dark waist-length hair was her crowning glory. She was Beattie's shadow, always there when she was needed and never complaining.

Come Christmastime, when the Salvation Army came to play carols, Beatrice was always sent out with a few coppers to put in their collection box. She stayed out for as long as she dared, enjoying their music and fascinated by the large shiny instruments and the pretty bonnets worn by the ladies. They seemed kind and cheerful people and Beatrice wished they came to Augusta Street more often. The week before Christmas, Bill put a little extra money on the kitchen table so that Beattie could invite her friends in to enjoy a glass of Christmas cheer. Not many were able to be as generous, so of course, it was a welcome treat and the mothers were delighted to be included in this homely get-together. The children did not expect more than an apple or an orange and perhaps some nuts, but they all looked forward to Christmas. They made decorations from scraps of coloured paper and stuck them together with flour and water.

The winters were often bitterly cold and coal was precious. Stew was kept hot hanging in a pot above the black sooty range, and throughout the week all sorts of leftovers were added. Stew was the backbone of every family's diet; it kept them going when the little meat ran out. The winter days were short on light and the sun didn't shine for long on the mean streets and grimy tenements of the East End, but the length of the working day never altered. Bill got up in the dark and came home in the dark, exhausted but grateful to be employed. Beattie would often say to the children, 'There's not an idle bone in your father's body'. He put new soles on their battered boots, even though their feet had sometimes outgrown them. They never went barefoot, which was no mean achievement. He was an altogether darling man!

All Change

Here's a penny whistle,
listen to my song.
My candle's shining brightly,
my hope forever strong.

The Industrial Revolution had changed so much:
the countryside; the cities and, in particular,
the inner cities; the working day; family life. Indeed,
there was nothing that had escaped the great hammer
blow of change. Whilst the wealthy industrialists
crowed about their marvellous achievements at
home and abroad, many families still existed in
dire circumstances. Certainly, the abysmally poor
stayed poor and lived in squalid housing that was
overrun with lice and vermin and had no proper
sanitation. It was not uncommon for a man to go to
work and not come home, having met with a fatal
accident in inadequate and unsafe factories. Sickness
claimed many lives at a time when doctors had to

be paid and few families could afford such luxury. Nevertheless, it has to be acknowledged that train travel, the invention of the underground railway and some better sewerage provision had a welcome impact on the lives of many. The docks were full of shipping from all over the world, the steel output was awesome and the cotton mills were thriving. Britain's amazing feats of engineering could not be overlooked. However, there was more than a glimmer of competition on the horizon. Whilst the nation basked in the glow of its great accomplishments, America and Germany were learning fast and Britain failed to recognise the signs. Export figures dropped a little and the shipbuilding yards saw a sudden falling-off in their order books. America had found a faster way of building ships and Germany was producing a whole range of products that caught the imagination and excitement of the entrepreneurs.

Annie and Maggie

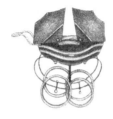

Cruel black are the days,
no star to light the sky.
Cry me a dirge
and see my babies die.

Towards the end of Queen Victoria's reign, after her stunning diamond jubilee, which was celebrated with a great show of affection and loyalty, Bill decided to move his family from Augusta Street, Poplar, to the countrified area of leafy Plaistow. Leaving behind the neighbours with whom they had shared so many hardships, they made the journey to May Road, set up home and started the next chapter in their lives.

The family soon acclimatised themselves to living in a new district. There were more trees in Plaistow and the roads were wider, with patches of green dotted here and there. There was space to breathe and space to play. The factories were not on their doorstep and it took a bus ride to get to the docks. Bill was pleased with the move. The future looked promising and he hoped that the family would thrive in this new environment.

And thrive they did, for as the saying goes, 'new house, new baby', and so it turned out, as Beattie announced her pregnancy in the summer of 1903. Needless to say, the news was welcomed, but a current of anxiety ran through the ensuing months. Bill was often heard to say, 'Sit down, Beat, the girls can do that', but his advice often fell on deaf ears: how can you put your feet up when you've got a hard-working husband, a house and four youngsters to care for? At this stage, Beatrice was nine, Bessie was seven, Billy was four and little Florence was just two years old.

On 28 September 1903, Beattie brought another set of twins into the world. They were two precious, albeit tiny girls, Annie Lilian and Margaret Ethel.

Life became desperately hard. Beattie did her best

to care, clean and cook, but Annie and Maggie were poorly babies and needed a lot of nursing. Young Beatrice was a godsend; she was often kept home from school to help her mother, who was almost at her wits' end with worry and tiredness. When Bill came home from work, Beatrice often wheeled the crying babies round the local park so her weary father could eat his dinner in a bit of peace. The man from the school board came knocking, enquiring about why Beatrice was not attending school and threatening to issue a summons if she did not return. Beattie spread her hands in despair. 'What can I do? I need her help!' The school board man shrugged and went away. Thankfully, they were given reprieve for another day – a small blessing in the miserable scheme of things.

The hard days and sleepless nights dragged on and they entered 1904 reeling through the grinding weariness of day-to-day living; yet worse was to come. Beattie's mother and grandmother were both poorly, and on 17 May the unimaginable happened: both mother and grandmother died, the first of TB and the second of bronchitis. Beattie was stunned by the two deaths on the same day. The loss was hard to bear, but tragedy had not yet finished with them.

In August that same year the twins succumbed to

epidemic diarrhoea and died within ten days of each other. Annie passed on 5 August, with Maggie following on the fifteenth. Beattie, in a state of utter anguish, tried to throw herself into the tiny grave, but she was pulled back sobbing and collapsed into Bill's arms.

The young Beatrice became the family's second mother. A shadowy Beattie existed on the edge of life. Bill left for work in the early mornings and spent his days in the belching workshops, longing to be home with Beattie. He and the children got used to the sound of muffled sobbing, and it was a long time before the whole family turned this harrowing corner. From the trauma of this crushing time, Bill moved his desolated wife and family to Queens Road, Plaistow.

Down the Frog and Toad to Number Seventeen Queens Road

Runny noses, frozen toes,
up and down the frog and toad.
Swinging lamps and costers' cries,
dear old Chrisp Street was alive

There was a new monarch on the throne. Edward VII, with the beautiful Alexandra and their six children by his side, ushered in the Edwardian age. The country approved of and admired Alexandra, especially noting how she doted on her children. Not surprisingly, the nation gobbled up the tittle-tattle that permanently hung around King Bertie. His giddy socialising and his hedonistic lifestyle were in complete contrast to the austere ways of Queen Victoria.

A new elegance adorned the world of fashion; the society ladies wore slender, often high-necked gowns, topped by the most extravagant hats, heavily loaded with feathers. Around their throats they wore collars of several strands of pearls: a direct steal from Queen Alexandra, who was often pictured wearing what was to become her own fashion statement. This was the period of the belle époque, as the French named it. It was also the time of the Gibson girl, introduced by the American artist Charles Dana Gibson. His conception of the newly emancipated woman was depicted in beautifully embroidered blouses with huge billowy sleeves, the necklines adorned with large floppy artists' bows. The fashion was taken up with great enthusiasm.

Young Beatrice, however, unimpressed by the glamour and with her heart firmly placed in the community, chose to 'sign the pledge' and join the Band of Hope, proudly singing 'Jesus Wants Me for a Sunbeam'. Signing the pledge was a promise to abstain from alcohol; this was certainly not a problem for Beatrice, who had grown up in an environment frequently blighted by the devastation of drink. The Band of Hope was formed in 1847 by Reverend

Jabez Tunnicliff, who had been very much affected by the untimely drink-related death of a young man. The movement aimed to teach the younger generation about the virtues of being teetotal.

Elizabeth, or 'catch-her-if-you-can Bessie', was of a different mettle. A fiery mixture of mischief and stubbornness and as quick-witted as they came, she was a character to be reckoned with: always the winner of an argument but often the cause of much laughter. Her lively brown eyes were never still and her long auburn hair was continually tossed in rebellion. 'Oh, Bessie!' was a constant cry.

The girls never argued about helping Beattie with the shopping. It was an entertainment that they relished. The atmosphere of the Saturday night market, with all its noise, colours and smells, was the highlight of their week. Bumping into neighbours, giggling at the saucy remarks of the costermongers, shuffling along past the stalls under the swinging lights of the market, they managed to forget their cold feet and runny noses. Now and again they came up against a copper, rocking on his heels on a street corner, his gaze raking the crowds for pickpockets and dodgy dealings. If they stood long enough by a stall, sometimes the girls heard the coster talking in a strange language to his mate. Bill told them this was rhyming slang, used to warn of possible danger to themselves or other traders – the sight of 'the law' unleashed a mouthful. The girls demanded to be taught some of these weird words and Bessie became proficient, using them whenever she could. It wasn't long before little Florence was escorted up the 'apples and pears', the baker's was up the 'frog and toad', and Billy got a playful cuff round the ear for calling his father 'me old china plate'.

Whilst King Bertie took mid-week and weekend breaks from reigning (and matrimony), the country bumbled along. Several significant events occurred: the suffragettes managed to disrupt the State opening of Parliament, a few more underground stations were opened and the Education (Provision of Meals) Act was passed, thereby enabling local education authorities to provide free meals to the poorest of children. In 1906 came the Workmen's Compensation Act, which gave workers entitlement to compensation for industrial injuries or diseases. This was widely applauded but disgracefully overdue. In the world of publishing, J. M. Dent, to much acclaim, established the Everyman Library with its first offering, James Boswell's The Life of Samuel Johnson. This year also spawned the publication of the much-loved story The Railway Children, which after more than a hundred years is still being read and cried over.

This was the background, then, to the lives of the Driscolls growing up in Plaistow. Bill was still working in the docks, Beattie was still trying to work her own brand of magic in the home, and the children were attending school. The regular comment that Beatrice, the eldest, heard was, 'Oh, Beatrice, if only you could do your arithmetic as well as you do your reading, writing and geography!' This was always accompanied by a deep sigh. Days off as mother's help had taken their toll.

Bessie digested everything easily, excelled in all her subjects and would have attended school on Saturday and Sunday had it been offered.

Billy – well, Billy dreamed, quietly did his sums, and drew and drew and drew. He drew at school, he drew at home and he drew on the pavement of Queens Road. He went to sleep with a pencil in his hand, his head full of ships.

Little Florence trailed after them all; her sweet nature and smiles were everyone's delight. When it was her time, she entered school without a qualm and just got on with it. They were settled at last.

In 1910 life and death caught up with King Bertie. After barely a decade on the throne he died, the last of the house of Saxe Coburg; now entered King

George V of Windsor and Queen Mary.

The Driscolls' household expenses were now being propped up with a little help from Beatrice, who had found employment with a lady who made exquisite silk flowers for stylish hats. Bessie was in her last year at school, working unpaid alongside her teacher with nowhere else to go, impatient to become fourteen and attend some other teaching establishment. Her need to learn was insatiable and beneath her bed was a pile of books that continued to grow. Shy Billy, often getting up with his father even when the stars were still in the sky, chattered on about faraway places and the sea routes that took the big ships there, always with a pencil in his hand. Beattie knew even then that there would come a time when she would be waiting on a letter and longing for the return of her only son.

The Great War, 1914

Out of the silence
a great singing.
Out of the carnage
a new beginning?

The newspapers were full of international incidents: an assassination, screaming headlines about dramas within the royal houses of Europe, the resultant crisis brought about by old treaties and, finally, the awful announcement of war.

The country was ill-prepared, but the Kaiser and Germany had been anticipating and preparing for becoming the masters of Europe, and Great Britain in particular. What a cousin! And so the slaughter began. Families were annihilated as husbands, fathers, brothers and sons went to fight for king and country and often didn't come back. Many of those who did return were wracked with shell shock, blinded or permanently blighted with lung disease from inhaling the killer gas. Beattie was thankful that Bill was too old and Billy too young.

Sweet William indeed, a dear boy loved by everyone, he could not be unkind. Billy was always smiling and was everybody's friend. His sisters adored him, as a baby and ever after. With deep blue eyes, thick light-brown wavy hair and a rather large pair of ears, he was earnest in all he did. Billy dreamed of big ships, drew big ships and yearned for foreign lands.

During this appalling time Bessie left school and, encouraged by her father, took herself off to night school and enrolled in courses for bookkeeping, shorthand and typing. In the company of like-minded students and guided by mostly female teachers (most of the staff had been men, but they were now fighting in the trenches) she thrived, even adding a few other subjects to her curriculum.

Billy went out of the front door at the crack of dawn with his father, staggering under the weight of a huge tool bag, which, according to his mother, was going to bring about a hernia. He had become an apprentice boiler-maker and found many encouraging hands around him, not only because he was so keen to learn but also because his father was a highly respected man. These were long and hard days for

Billy, but he seldom complained; he had entered the world of ships and shipbuilding.

Not Quite Kosher

Then came Abraham from afar
on his Turkish carpet
under David's star.

B essie by now had launched herself on to the first rung of the commercial ladder and taken herself and her talents to an office in Aldgate. Here she typed, made the tea and meticulously filed the day away, attending her bookkeeping classes in the evening and conquering the pot hooks and hangers of Pitman shorthand.

As the time passed, Bessie's confidence grew and

so did her admirers, although Bill was wont to say, 'Not one of you girls is as beautiful as your mother; she was the pride of Millwall.' There could never be another Beattie, and Bill still adored her.

Towards the end of the war, Bessie began to 'walk out' with a young man named Gus, and Bill and Beattie took to him. He was a steady, reliable fellow and had a regular job in the docks; he was one of their own and totally acceptable. Bessie's prospects bloomed with her growing achievements, and she applied for another post in the city and added bookkeeping and shorthand to her daily duties.

With the arrival of the jazz age and Alexander's Ragtime Band, the girls were sent giddy. Although Bill tried to put his foot down and forbade them to go to extremes, they bobbed their hair and became thoroughly modern. They shortened their dresses, donned the shoes of the moment and tried to disguise their bosoms. They flapped their way into the twenties and one evening they danced their way through the long, much prized mirror that graced the end of the passage. There was hell to pay at the time, but, as usual, all was soon forgiven and the girls continued to flash their legs as they charlestoned, black-bottomed and turkey-trotted all over the house. One day, Billy delighted them by bringing home a wonderful wind-up gramophone. The house rang with music and laughter. Beattie loved it and encouraged it all, but Bill put his hands over his ears, taking his Guinness into the back yard. It was a happy and exhilarating time, and they relished it.

One evening, Bessie came home and told them that the chairman of the carpet company for whom she worked had called her into his office and informed her that he wanted her to work with his new business partner, who had recently arrived in London from Turkey and spoke very little English. The chairman wanted Miss Driscoll to work alongside his partner until he became more acquainted with the language. Bessie saw this as a promotion and indeed, her salary was increased. The gentleman arrived and Bessie took him under her wing. She did his correspondence, taught him English and popped out to buy his lunch. Albert (for that was his name) brought her thank-you chocolates and flowers and took her to dinner. Eventually, he bought her a ring. The chairman was delighted; her father was incandescent with rage. Albert was a Jew. Albert was, in fact, Abraham – a widower with children. Poor Gus became a back number. Life at 17 Queens Road became unbearable. Never had the Driscolls known such division. Father barely spoke to mother, daughter Bessie cried and her sisters and brother Billy walked on eggshells. Eventually, Bessie quietly left. Number seventeen was a sombre place; they all missed her sparkling presence.

Beatrice was now a mother's help to a publican's wife, and her charges were little Percy and Connie. She was happy in the household and much appreciated. The children were firmly attached to her and most days and nights she had sole charge of them. They took trips up the river, had picnics in the park and enjoyed holidays at the seaside; the landlady, their mother, was the epitome of fashion with her coiffured hair and her exotic outfits, and Beatrice had many an amusing tale to tell when she came home on an occasional day off. At this time all things Egyptian were the rage, and the lady of the house dressed accordingly, passing from lounge through to bars in harem trousers and a multitude of bangles. She smoked her scented cigarettes in a long, elegant holder and her use of cosmetics was nothing short of theatrical.

During one of their many seaside holidays, Beatrice and the children went crabbing and filled a bucket with the sideways-inclined creatures. At the end of the day they returned to their cottage and, at Percy's insistence, took the bucket with them. After tea and trying to wash the sand out from between the children's toes, Beatrice finally got them into bed; soon after, she gratefully put her head on her pillow. She was awakened in the wee small hours by a strange clattering sound and, sitting up in bed, she saw by the light of a bright moon eight crabs scuttling about. She shrieked and drew her knees up to her chest, desperately trying to think of what to do next, but the decision was made for her. Percy noisily awoke from a dream and called for her, and when she didn't immediately cross the room to comfort him, he stepped on to the floorboards and padded his sleepy way towards her. By this time Connie had joined in and Beatrice had to act. She plonked Percy on to her bed, charged across to the door and flung it wide, hoping the crabs would escape to sandy freedom. But Percy, now wide awake and aware, was having none of it. He wanted those crabs back in the bucket to take home. Chaos ensued. Beatrice grabbed one of the crabbing nets and frantically proceeded to capture the wayward creatures and dump them back into the bucket, filling it with tap water and depositing it outside the front door. Percy hollered, Connie joined in and Beatrice, for once, wished for the company of another grown-up. It was still only three o'clock in the morning. In pyjamas and beach shoes they left the cottage, Beatrice trying to turn it into an adventure by explaining that the crabs needed their mummy and were trying to get home. Only slightly mollified, the children trudged to the jetty and upturned the bucket, whereupon all the silvery shining crabs slid into the water and disappeared. Connie clapped her hands and said 'Gone!' but Percy turned and stomped back to bed. Beatrice wondered if he would ever forgive her. He did, of course, and he enjoyed retelling the story many times after.

After leaving school Florence was employed in a local shirt factory. She was close enough to come home at mid-day for a bite to eat and to sit with the cat on her lap whilst she read her latest copy of The People's Friend. Beattie's constant reminder, 'Watch the clock, Florrie!' often fell on deaf ears, and most days it ended with Florrie flying out of the front door with a piece of cake in her hand. Billy had joined the navy and was working hard for commendations on his papers. Bill was proud of his son but silently grieved for his absent daughter.

In the autumn of 1923 Bessie appeared in her finery, diamond rings on her fingers and moving in a cloud of expensive perfume. She brought with her gifts and she brought with her news. She was pregnant, and Albert was overjoyed. Beattie's mind was in turmoil. How was she to break the news to Bill, and how could she hide her own delight? Bessie, proud and brave in her new family status, faced her father and, with dignity, calmly asked for his forgiveness and blessing. Bill looked at her hard and finally nodded his head, his eyes bright with unshed tears. In 1922 Nassim came shouting into the world, to be followed two years later by beautiful Esthriah. These two healthy children gladdened Beattie's heart. Albert doted on them and they and Bessie were feted with the best that money could buy.

There were occasions when Beattie was embarrassed by Bessie's arrival in Queens Road, loaded with treats and dressed in the latest fashion. The fancy hats and furs were out of place in the street and Beattie, never one for show, usually hustled her daughter through the front door.

Comings and Goings

Tears and joy,
sometimes summer sand,
a lemonade or
holding someone's hand.
That first-time moon,
the shimmering stars,
a broken heart
in a penny jar.

In the meantime, Beatrice had been introduced to Walter Levett and they began to keep company when her duties would allow. He was easy-going and adaptable, mixing in with the family, and the sisters found him amusing. Although certainly a few years older than Beatrice, the age difference didn't seem to lessen their friendship and they jogged along companionably. They visited music halls, took trips to the seaside and even went to the races once or twice.

Then Florence met dashing Bert Fisher, who soon became a regular visitor to number seventeen. Once he had attained the rank of second engineer, wedding bells rang out and Florence Driscoll became Florence Fisher. Time was moving on.

Bessie often came with her children and took Beattie for days out. They jaunted to Westcliffe, to Brighton and to Hove, and sampled the little luxuries that Albert provided. Beattie sat on the promenade with the children at her feet and revelled in their constant chatter. Beatrice was still keeping company with Walter. Walter loved a gamble and kept a little notebook in which he jotted down the horse-racing odds. He always had a 'certainty' but Billy and Bert soon learnt not to listen, for Walter's stock phrase 'You'll be sorry' seldom came true, but old Bill's did – 'Walter, the only winner is the bookie'. Walter supported West Ham and always attended the home games, nipping into The Boleyn pub for a quick one before the kick-off. He proved to be a lively mimic of many a stage act, and the sisters encouraged his antics. He certainly knew how to entertain and was welcome at many gatherings. He was known as 'a bit of a lad'.

Florence gave birth to Pamela Elsie and they duly joined the family outings, with Bert Fisher accompanying them when his boat came home. Beattie's old premonition about Billy's wanderings was fulfilled, but he was a kind and thoughtful son who wrote regularly from whatever port he was in. He was still in love with the big ships and the sea. For Billy, there was always another horizon.

Beatrice was still walking out with Walter. One summer Beatrice, now in her late thirties, took herself off to seek employment in the guesthouses around the seaside resorts of southern England. Beattie and Bill received postcards and commentaries, biscuits and cream, but no news of Walter. Bessie and Florrie anxiously awaited the end of the holiday season, when they felt sure that Beatrice would return with some happy news. It never happened. Sure, Beatrice came home, but by then it had become obvious that Beattie's health was ailing and she needed help at home. The girls rallied round, taking turns to cook and do housework and keeping a weather eye on Bill, who in turn watched Beattie grow frailer by the month. The doctor came and went, then came again, and his face was grave. His prescriptions made little difference other than cruelly raising their hopes. Beattie's pain and frustration was sometimes vented on them through the old stock comment, 'Oh, don't make a fuss!' but soon that fell by the wayside and she spent longer in bed and could eat very little. They tried to tempt her with fancy morsels, but she brushed them aside and complained about the cooking smells that wafted up the stairs.

The winter months closed in and Christmas loomed closer, but an awful bleakness hung over the house. The half-anticipated cancer had become a reality and finally, the doctor drew them together and spoke the words that none of them wanted to hear: 'You may have your mother until Christmas, but I'm afraid it's doubtful'. It wasn't to be. Beattie closed her eyes on 21 December 1931 and the world stopped turning for the Driscolls.

After the funeral they sat round the old kitchen table and Bill looked at their ashen faces. With a tear-streaked face, clutching a whisky in his fist, he raised his jaw and said, 'We can do no more for the dead; now we must look after the living'.

Playtime in Priory –
Back to the Half Pint

A scrappy kid
inclined to roam
but all those streets
led back to home.
No door locked,
the world a friend,
how lucky I was
Amen, amen.

The arrival of a baby at number seventeen must have set the neighbours gossiping; can't you just imagine it? What a gift amongst the teacups I must have been, a titbit to tide them over through the perishing January and a little further before the novelty wore off. My mother hated it. Although 1934 was considered, at least on the surface, to be thoroughly modern, old notions and ideals of morality lingered and nowhere more so than at number seventeen. How old Bill's fingers must have itched to take off the Driscoll belt, not infrequently threatened in the past. But realising that he would be confronting a middle-aged man and an already devastated daughter, he was heard to question in a sad and soulful voice, 'Oh, Walter, what have you done? ' The aunts went into a huddle, Billy sailed for Japan and Grandad continued to twang his braces. The aunts were good and did their sisterly bit, closing rank and providing support, although they were almost as mystified by the turn of events as my poor mother, who maintained the belief that the menopause had come early. Some menopause. It surely was a change of life for all of them. My father reluctantly looked for rooms and eventually our threesome ended up in Manor Park, predictably on the wrong side of the railway track. Grandad and Uncle Billy coped as best as they could with the help of my aunts.

I grew, apparently, into a scrawny kid, who survived somehow on 'fresh air pudding' and Tizer. My main diet, when I could be persuaded to sit still long enough to eat, was haddock, watercress, bits of bacon and the odd sip of Grandad's Guinness. Oh, how I loved my grandad; when he came to visit he lit up my day and my mum laughed.

The precocious Shirley Temple was still a favourite and was idolised on both sides of the Atlantic. This was the golden age of Hollywood, when the stars shone the brightest, the ladies were the most beautiful, the men were impossibly handsome and the musicals were the most extravagant. Everyone flocked to the cinema for an injection of escapism and glamour. I was taken to the pictures to see anything that moved, and sure enough, by the age of four I was the proud possessor of a pair of red beribboned tap-dancing shoes and enrolled at Peggy O'Farrell's Dancing School somewhere in East Ham, preparing to become one of the Little Tappers. I never went to bed with the sweet sound of Golden Slumbers lulling me to sleep, but I regularly nodded off to the current hits of Flanagan and Allen.

One glorious Christmas my dad pushed the boat out and took Mum and me 'up west' to the Coliseum to see a pantomime. The theatre took my breath away even before the performance began. The smell of cigars, the fancy clothes of the audience, the lights and the high staircase – for me it was all pure magic. We sat in a box, my mother wearing her fox stole (smelling of mothballs) and my father sipping Johnnie Walker from his hip flask. During the performance, he struck up some sort of repartee with the on-stage villain and my mother died a thousand deaths, but I was in heaven and sobbed when the house lights came up and it was time to go home. I remember kneeling on the taxi seat and through a mist of tears watching that wonderful silver ball on top of the Coliseum go round.

Not surprisingly, like other children who live in somewhat discordant situations, I quickly realised that our family was a bit different. For starters, my mother was in her forties and my father his fifties, both old enough to be my grandparents. My mother, bless her, was always fiercely protective and would have wrapped me in cotton wool, but my aunts, now both seasoned mothers, tried diplomatically to infer that this was not a good idea. Anyway, as they said, she would have to catch me first; they tell I was almost running before I could walk. Indeed, early photographs depict me being firmly held down by a grown-up or a cousin and glowering at the camera.

There seemed to be times when my dad was absent, maybe visiting his sister or at the pub with his cronies. There were times when we didn't play happy families, and there were many times when the silence was as deafening as a beating drum, and I hated it. I believe that it was around this time that my grandad became a man of property and purchased a little house in Priory Road in East Ham: Beehive Cottage, I think. My Auntie Florrie and Cousin Pam moved in, and Uncle Bert went to sea. It seemed to me that Uncle Bert and Uncle Billy were always going or returning, but every trip heralded a present for me. I remember a pretty bamboo sunshade and a dolly's tea set from Japan. Their return was always a great occasion. They had such tales to tell; the kettle was always on and the Guinness flowed. Pam and I sat under the table loving every minute of it – until a grown-up realised it was past our bedtimes, and then it was up the stairs to 'Bedfordshire'.

When Uncle Bert's ship was berthed for repairs at Sheerness, Auntie Florrie and Pam had to up-sticks and move to the Isle of Sheppey; and so it was that the Levett trio took over 80 Priory Road. My mother was glad to be out of rooms, and with Grandad as landlord we were safe and secure. I was overjoyed to live in a little house where the stairs were shut away behind a cupboard door, with a patch of garden at the back and an outside lavvy, where a resident big black spider lurked in the creeping ivy. We discovered good, kind and especially colourful neighbours, whose language was full of words that were foreign to me but more than hair-raising to my mother. Of course, I quickly added them to my fast-expanding vocabulary and proudly trotted them out, especially to Grandad, who let them all slide over his head without batting an eyelid.

Despite this change of circumstance, my mother and father did not grow closer together. They were better apart. It was almost a relief when my dad went off to work. True, my mother sometimes scowled her way through the day and often beat the daylights out of the scullery mat, but her wrath was never vented on me. I soon learned when to keep out of the way of both of them, especially when the in-house temperature rose. Happily, there were other occasions when we did joined-up things – maybe going to Southend for the day, when I was unleashed to run down the pier or visit Peter Pan's Playground. I recall bus trips out to Epping Forest and Wanstead Flats, when we took roast-beef sandwiches and ate them on the top deck, but even those days had an edgy feel about them and I waited for the bubble to burst. I journeyed through my childhood better prepared than any boy scout.

Of course, much later I discovered the reason for all this angst. My father had married as a very young man and his even younger wife had run off to Australia with an uncle. Uncle! Now there's a relation who covers a multitude of sins. A few years down the line, when he met my mother, he overlooked mentioning that he was married and for a decade they walked out together. My mother waited for him to pop the question, but it didn't come (well, certainly not the right one), and by this time she was keeping house for Grandad and younger brother Billy, beloved Nana Driscoll having died a couple of years earlier. When the spanner in the works arrived, my father had to come clean and so the search was on to prove whether he would be a bigamist by marrying my mother. Eventually, my mother got the ring and a baby, but in the wrong order. They stuck together in a strange relationship and, looking back, I suppose I was probably the jam in the sandwich.

The move to Priory Road proved to be the opening up of all sorts of excitement for me. From the age of three, what I lacked in brothers and sisters I made up for in friends. I quickly linked up with the Norcotts, the Averys and the Pollentines; where they went, I went too – no escapade too naughty, no street too far. I became a roamer, always more out than in, and the promise 'She'll be all right with us, Missus' was true; I always was. There were two star attractions in Priory, an entry into Upton Park football ground

(West Ham) and a bus garage. Usually, once a week someone would say, 'Let's go up the garridge!' so we did. Trailing past the neat pocket-hankie-sized front gardens, we'd make our way to the forbidden territory, where the red buses loomed large and exciting and the drivers and conductors lounged about reading their Daily Mirror and smoking. We were greeted with the customary welcome, 'Op it, you kids!' So we 'opped it onto a bus when we thought they weren't looking and hid on the top deck. Sure that we hadn't been spotted, we crouched down as the bus throbbed into life and made its way along Priory until it reached the end of the road. Then it stopped, and a voice would holler up the stairs, 'All right, you lot – off!' and we'd all come scuttling down. Someone would always shout 'Thanks, guv'nor!' the bell would ting and the bus would turn into the traffic on the main road. We collected the old bus tickets and the older ones amongst us swapped them and used them for all sorts of games.

One day when we were mooching about we discovered a loose plank in the fence that enclosed part of the football ground. With a bit of gentle persuasion, one of the boys made it big enough for us to squeeze through and we found ourselves in a new world. We were underneath the stands in a deserted, dusty and semi-lit new play area, not far from what was to become the Trevor Brooking end. This was a grand find, and a new way for the older boys to bunk in and watch a home game. These were the days I loved the most: some of the neighbours rented out their patchy front yards so supporters could leave their bicycles in safety whilst they watched the match; other neighbours made tea and sold it over their front window sills, trading raucous comments with the customers. It was busy, it was noisy, it was bliss, and we kids dodged in and out of all of it. Priory Road was alive.

Sometimes the jam-jar man turned up, carrying his roundabout on the back of his large cart. We got a ride on the roundabout if we gave him a clean jam jar, so collecting jars became a matter of extreme competition. If one of us heard that the old fellow was a couple of streets away, we would dash indoors and plague our mothers until they scoured the cup-boards and came up with as many jars as they could find. I have to say that if we saw someone from another street queuing up, we weren't very neigh-bourly and weren't beyond elbowing him or her out of the way. Territory was territory, after all.

Grandad extended his property portfolio and

snapped up a semi-detached house in Falconwood Avenue, Welling – over the other side of the river. This journey entailed a trip on the number 101 bus and then – oh, joy! – a jaunt on the ferry boat across to Woolwich. Once off the ferry we caught the number 696 trolleybus to Welling Corner. During this part of the trip I always felt sick and usually arrived in insipid Welling a bit green around the gills. Mum gushed on about the fresh air and the quietness, but the novelty soon wore off. There were rows upon rows of lookalike houses, shining windows and dainty curtains, and every front door was most firmly shut. Into this land of 'don't touch' my Auntie Florrie moved, so our trips became regular outings that were highlighted by the chug across the water and the excitement of watching the boat's huge brass engines go round. The trolley-buses were a recent addition to the transport scene and fairly purred along, but not infrequently the arm fell off the top cabling system and everything stopped whilst the driver reached up with a long pole to hook the bus on to its line again.

Back in the land of semi-normality, things ticked over. Dad went to work in the docks as a grain clerk and his hours and wages were regular; we lived a comfortable if not flush life. By then I had acquired a few more aunts and uncles and a couple of girl cousins from the Levett side. The cousins were much older than I, so they were no good as playing companions, but we didn't see them very often so it wasn't much of a disappointment. However, a trip 'up west' to spend a day with Auntie Bessie and my cousins Essie and Nassim, who was now nicknamed Bubby (Essie couldn't get her tongue around 'brother') was always eagerly anticipated. They were very different and involved me in all sorts of welcome mischief. The bumpy, noisy ride on the number eleven bus out to Shepherd's Bush was exciting, lurching through unfamiliar streets, passing huge shops and massive blocks of flats, then finally getting off at The Green and tripping down Pennard Road. Once inside the front door I was swept off my feet in a bear hug and enveloped in an aroma of Midnight in Paris perfume and exotic cooking odours.

There was nowhere else like Auntie Bessie's house. Lights that came on with the touch of a switch, doors that folded back to reveal other rooms and pretty wall lamps that made the rooms seem extra cosy and welcoming. Then there was Uncle Albert, a wonder in himself. His dark eyes twinkled behind his owl-like glasses and a chuckle was always ready on his lips. Seldom was he without a fistful of chocolate for us all. Bubby brought out his ever-increasing train set to show, and Essie had a magical dressing-up cupboard filled with sparkly high heels and shimmering dresses left over from Auntie Bessie's flapper days and (mostly) nights. We clopped around, tripping over our long dresses and trying on bits of discarded jewellery, wandering through a world of wonderful make-believe. We often sat down to a meal of kiftikas and fried potatoes, whilst Uncle Albert smoked his Sobranie cigarettes and told us outrageous stories. Who wouldn't have loved them?

Occasionally in Priory Road there appeared a strange and alarming man who strode about ranting and raving, waving his arms high in the air whilst all the time his long, ragged coat flapped around him. We kids played a dare game, trying to get as close to him as we could, but all the while being scared he would turn on us. We called him Mad Mop. My grandad witnessed the antics of this creature on several visits and one day took me aside, sat me down and explained the reason for this weird behaviour. He certainly made me feel ashamed of myself and I never joined in this game thereafter. Mop – we never knew his real name – had been a soldier in the Great War of 1914 and he was still suffering from shell shock. He had suffered terrible head wounds and the hospital doctors had put a metal plate in his head to fill the gap where half his scalp had been blown away. Grandad said he would never get better. I remember the silence that followed this explanation.

When the days grew longer and the sun shone, we sometimes caught the train to Benfleet. It was a thrill putting some pennies into the chocolate machine on the station platform and pulling out a mauve packet of Cadbury's chocolate, which I munched as the stations flew by. Trees and fields, cows and sheep were witnessed and stored to be thought about later in a mist of sleepiness on the return journey. Benfleet. Over the bridge on a green bus to Canvey Island, past the little gaily painted boats stuck drunkenly on the mud, waiting for the tide to turn. Heaven! First stop, a tea shed; second stop, the bucket-and-spade shop; third stop, over the sea wall and down to the beach. On one amazing occasion, Dad paddled with me. I can't remember whether that was before or after his trip to the Haystack pub, but it was still a major event. One year we even stayed in a dear house on May Avenue, which boasted a veranda. From here, we could see the water and watch the boats go by. In the evenings Mum told me stories about the Dutchmen who sailed to Canvey and tried to build canals and houses resembling those they had left behind in their own watery country. She was good at stories, my mum. She fired my determination to read as soon as I could.

There was a little shop in Priory Road called Batiste's. Was that the correct spelling? I can't be sure, but it was a place of delights with three high steps that led us into a world of nose-twitching smells and shady treasures. It was like a second home to all the kids who flocked there to spend their ha'pennies and sit on the steps to swap jelly babies and aniseed balls. Piled up on the floor in front of the shining wooden counter were large square silver tins full of biscuits of all varieties and, most importantly, the special tin that contained all the broken offerings. From the ceiling hung long sausages dressed in netting and on the counter sat a large set of scales with all the weights stacked up alongside it. Butter, suet, cheese, bacon and just about everything else went the way of the scales, and all the while there was constant chatter across the counter as current gossip was exchanged. Here was the 1930s equivalent of social services; a trouble shared was indeed a trouble halved. It did go via the whole of Priory Road, but let it be said that no one was overlooked and no one was left without help. No form filling, but plenty of cups of tea and well-meaning advice. But best of all, as far as we kids were concerned, was the fact that the biscuits were low enough to pinch – and we did.

From May onwards the water-ice man came down the road, pedalling his cart, and from inside the big box on the back he produced delicious water ices of all flavours. He tinged his bell and stopped in the middle of the road; front doors flew open, kids and dogs made a ring round him and his trade was fierce and brisk. Most of the time the ice was handed over in spills of newspaper; now and again he was presented with a dish, but it still got the newspaper treatment. Mostly we sat on our front doorsteps and slurped it down. It didn't take long but my, it was lovely on a hot summer's day.

As it got nearer to Christmas, we ventured through the portals of the bigger shops and the departmental emporiums. We wandered through the various sections, touching, sniffing, oohing and ahhing until we were satiated with the extravagance of it all. Tins of fancy food, glacé fruits, Belgian chocolates, packaged perfumes, silk stockings and then, finally, the fairyland grotto, that magical place, strung with lights and dotted with nodding elves and fairies. Our joy was complete when we spotted 'himself', sitting in a corner, emblazoned in red, with a huge white curly beard, little round glasses on the tip of his nose and twinkling eyes, encouraging all the children to step up and tell him their Christmas hopes and dreams. He reminded me of Uncle Albert. The glossy reindeers were parked nearby, waiting for the night-time getaway. Oh, those Christmases of the late 1930s were such special times!

In May 1937, we had a right royal knees-up in Priory Road. It was a special occasion because we were getting a new king and queen, as well as two princesses. Everyone seemed to be very pleased about this. The king we had had for a very short while, Edward, had decided he didn't want to do it any more (well, not on his own) and Grandad told me that something called Parliament didn't like his lady friend, so they made him choose between her and staying king. He had chosen her. So here we were, having a grand street party with cake, jelly and funny hats. Grandad and Uncle Billy were there and helped put up the tables and set out the chairs. Then everyone hung flags and bunting over the houses. My dad helped with the tablecloths, cups, saucers, plates and glasses. Old Mrs Smith wore a tea towel over her shoulder in case she spotted a mucky plate.

It was like Christmas in summertime. The wireless poured out happy music and every now and then a posh man told us what was happening 'up west'. All the kids wore paper hats and some had put on special fancy clothes; one boy was dressed up as a jockey. I wore a silk Union Jack pinafore, a red, white and blue hair ribbon and my wellington boots. Mrs Smith had found me a green hat, but it kept falling off.

It was very noisy and exciting, and we kids ran in and out of the tables, getting in everyone's way. Then we all had to line up to have our photograph taken. Rosie Norcott and I were made to stand in front because we were the smallest. It took a long time before everyone was in place, so Mr Bosher hung on to me in case I did a bunk, which was, in fairness, highly likely. My hat blew away again and Mrs Smith bent down to catch it, just at the moment when the photographer clicked the shutter. Anyway, we all had a happy time and when it got dark the grown-ups danced in the street and drank their beer. When I went to bed I remember hoping that the two prin-cesses, Elizabeth and Margaret Rose, had enjoyed themselves as much as I had. Later my mum bought me a lovely toy golden coronation coach with horses strung out in front.

More excitement came in August when I got a

Confined to School

A caged little birdie
with soggy wet drawers,
but still on the next day
got sent back for more.

In September 1938, I was dragged screaming and kicking into school. Through a gate, behind railings, I was deposited in a playground with a lot of other kids (some peaceful, others not so willing), made to line up and told to follow a teacher when the bell was rung. The bell went, the line moved forward and I did a runner. Unfortunately, my mum was still there, and she adroitly nobbled my escape. Halfway across the playground we were met by a lady with frizzy orange hair, who prised me off my mother's legs, pulled me into a room and kicked shut the door. Here we sized each other up. According to her, we were going to have a lovely day doing all sorts of exciting things. But it never happened! I had a knicker problem. Halfway through the morning, I needed to go. An obliging girl took me by the hand and led me across the playground to the toilet block, and told me she would wait outside. Then – disaster! My mother had sewn my knicker elastic too tight. I couldn't pull them down, so not surprisingly, after struggling for a bit I wet them. I started to wail but no one came. With soggy, smelly knickers, I tried to escape but found I couldn't reach the door latch. The 'obliging girl' had given up on me and gone back to her class, and everyone had forgotten all about me.

At some stage, Orange Hair must have realised that I was missing and sent out a search party. The 'obliging girl' owned up to abandoning me in the toilet block and so I was eventually rescued, me and my Cambridge-blue knickers. Oh, the kneeling cuddles I got, the wiping of my nose, the drying of my eyes. At last, they let go of me and I managed to kick a few shins.

Towards the end of the year, we three took a trip to London proper. This time it was on a bus that wove past Westminster Abbey and the Army and Navy stores and deposited us outside the Victoria Palace Theatre, the home of the Crazy Gang. Sure, we had the atmosphere, the lights and the music, but as I looked around I saw that the audience was very short on children. Truth to tell, there was a lot of talking, raucous laughter and some whistling. The Crazy Gang with Nervo and Knox were obviously favourites of my dad's, but I didn't come to life until Flanagan and Allen entered from the wings. Out they strolled, one behind the other, Bud Flanagan wearing his ridiculously long moth-eaten fur coat and his squashed soft hat and Chesney Allen immaculately suited, topped by a rakishly tipped trilby. The audience roared their approval as the pair launched into 'The Umbrella Man'. Bud beamed across the orchestra pit, his dark, roguish eyes making connections this way and that, whilst Ches never took his hand off his partner's shoulder. They were the stars of the show, and they brought the house down and the audience to its feet with 'Underneath the Arches'. I loved them. There was a fizz about them, especially Bud Flanagan, and I can still picture his dear rubbery old face. I seem to recall some very underdressed ladies hopping around the stage, but they weren't worth staying awake for.

Something Afoot

No one depends
upon

my new red bike
a trike

smudged with mud
small clots

except for me
ESCAPE

There was something going on! My grandad was doing a lot of talking to my mum and dad, and it seemed to be important, serious stuff. They often listened to the man on the wireless. Uncle Billy was just as serious when he called. I didn't understand, but I didn't like the sound of it. I hated seeing them all so gloomy.

In January, I had my fifth birthday and things cheered up a bit. Mum and I trooped down to Lant's Toy Shop and returned home with me pushing a shiny blue-and-cream bassinet doll's pram. The fat white tyres were shrouded in corrugated brown wrapping paper and the wintry sun sparkled on the chrome of the shade levers and the handle bar. It was an elegant thing all right, and my mother loved it. It took pride of place in the outhouse and no one was allowed to touch it except me. I pushed it up and down Priory Road and the other kids wanted to lift the shade and put the brake on. I was urged never to leave it unattended, but I have to say it seriously interfered with my other activities. I couldn't really take it up to the garage and certainly not through the hole in the West Ham fence. It was useful for a trip to the chippy or to the off-licence with Grandad to carry home his Guinness, but I was not a good mother to the various dolls that came my way, those with the pink faces, blonde hair and open-and-shut blue eyes. The only doll I really liked was a little black one with chubby legs and a smiley face – and, of course, my special teddy bear, a gift from Auntie Bessie.

So the pram began to languish somewhat and my most prized possession became my red three-wheeler bike, which I rode round Central Park like a kid possessed and came off with monotonous regularity. No number of scabbed knees and grazed elbows dented my enthusiasm. One day, however, I resurrected the pram and pushed it into the back yard. At one end I sat my teddy and at the other my little black doll, covering them with a pretty blanket. I walked them around the wallflowers until I felt a spot of rain. I quickly rearranged them and pressed the lever to put up the shade, catching my fingers in the spring. It hurt. I yelled, and my mother came rushing out of the scullery just in time to see me aim a vicious kick at the body of the pram. She was horrified! I was dragged indoors and shoved up the stairs behind the cupboard, and all the while she hollered after me what a nasty and ungrateful girl I was. Doubtless she was right, but strangely that pram had always meant more to her than it had to me.

Grandad, my Grandad

DON'T give me presents
DON'T buy me sweets
DON'T hold my hand
as we walk down the street.
Today this day is very black,
please, Mary, send my grandad back.

My grandad had stopped coming to visit. So we made the trip on the ferry to Auntie Florrie, with whom he was living. My roly-poly jolly grandad was not so jolly any more, and he was spending longer in the little downstairs room off the hall. Mum and Auntie Florrie were really worried about him and Dr Cochrane became a regular visitor; Auntie Bessie arrived with her usual bag of lovely food and presents for everyone, but this time even her magic didn't work. Grandad sank lower and lower. Then someone turned the lights out – my grandad died and my world collapsed. It was Easter 1939. There was no one to call me 'Eiley Wiley', no one's pockets to rifle for sweets and sandwiches, and no more walking over the bumps at the end of Welling Way. Everything changed.

I stood between my big cousins at the number 160 bus stop; they towered over me and Olive tightly gripped my hand as we waited to go to Grove Park to spend the day with Auntie Lizzie, my dad's sister. They had said that this was a special day for Grandad and the grown-ups had lots of things to do. I remember looking across the road at a statue of a little lady and asking who she was. 'Mary', they said. She was standing in the garden of a special school, Maryville Convent. The number 160 came along and we went upstairs. Mary was still there when we came back, and was for many years. I liked it that she was close to where Grandad had been.

The Blitz

'Bang, bang!'
the Hitler man said,
'You're dead!'
'Oh yeah' was the reply,
'You're in for a surprise!'

Later that year my mum and dad sat with their heads close to the wireless, listening to a very gloomy man. When he stopped speaking some solemn music came on. They switched the music off and my mum went out to the kitchen to put the kettle on whilst my dad rolled up a smoke. No one spoke. The street was strangely quiet. I looked out. No Rosie, no Johnny and not a Pollentine in sight.

Eventually, my dad spoke. 'Well, that's it, Beat.' War had been declared. I didn't understand.

Next day the sun shone, the buses went up and down Priory, and the milkman gave me his box of old stubby pencils. I treasured these blunt bits and pieces and used them all the time when I played shops. I never swapped them, no matter what was on offer, and I frequently had one lodged behind my ear. I wrote on any paper that came my way and my little desk drawer overflowed with sheets of scribble.

School was just about all right, but it was a waste of time when the sun shone and I wanted to be out and about. And the sun did shine during that September; it was warm, the skies were blue and it was great to whizz up and down Priory on my new scooter. Then odd things started to happen. A van turned up in the street and all the mums were called outside to watch a demonstration of something called a stirrup pump. Even my mum had to have a go. One by one, they all struggled to hold the thing up whilst water was jetted on to a make-believe fire. Of course, there was plenty of laughter and a few kids got deliberately wet, so it turned out to be quite a good afternoon.

Not long after this, serious people arrived on the doorstep asking lots of questions and filling in forms.

My mum called them nosey parkers and closed the door, but they kept coming back. They wanted to know if she would consider having me evacuated. The short answer to that was 'No!' I hung about behind the door and wondered what 'evacuated' meant. It sounded nasty. The people were persistent and in the end I heard Mum say, 'If one of us goes, we all go!' Go? Go where? Bang! went the front door again.

But after that doorstep interview even more unusual things began to happen. Mr Bosher next door flattened his back garden and dug a great big hole over which he built an air-raid shelter; around the doorway he stacked lots of sandbags and on the roof he put slabs of grassy earth. We were given gas masks, horrible large smelly rubber things to strap over our faces, to protect us from breathing in poison gas. What was that? Then Mum had to buy some black material to cover our windows at night so that our gaslight couldn't be seen from the outside. In an odd way, to me it felt exciting. The man on the wireless warned about air raids; street names disappeared and street lights didn't light. If people needed to be out after dark, they were told to keep a torch in their pocket. Then we were introduced to the sound of the air-raid siren. There was nothing exciting about that; indeed, a few short months later its wail sent a bucket of cold water down my back. It was the sound that told you that in a few minutes from now, you could be dead.

Dads, uncles, sons and brothers were called up to join the armed forces; the men who were too old stayed behind and were encouraged to 'dig for victory'. Vegetables appeared everywhere.

Then it was the turn of the ladies. Because so many agricultural workers had been taken off the land to fight, the Women's Land Army was formed. Mum was given ration books to use when she went shopping and suddenly, sweets were 'off'. A lot more things became 'off' as time went on, and what wasn't off certainly didn't fill the cupboard. Then Mum was issued with clothing coupons.

After the first air raid on London, I knew what being at war was all about.

In between times everyone tried to carry on doing the usual things: going to work, going to school, family visits. Sometimes people stumbled to the pictures or the pub in the dark, but always making sure their blackout curtains were light-proof first. On one occasion, we even braved a trip on the Woolwich Ferry to visit Auntie Florrie in Welling. It was a bit of an adventure, with us dreading the siren going and then hoping the trolleybus was functioning, but we got there, the kettle went on and Mum and Auntie Florrie got down to some serious gossiping. Teatime and blackout time came, then the chance for me on the way back from the lavatory to have a quick explore in the front room. Just inside the door was a light switch. With fascination (remember, we only had gaslight in Priory), I pushed it down and the room was flooded with light. I pressed it up – darkness. I had another go and looked around. Pictures on the wall, a piano, ornaments and even some flowers. This was some style! I pushed the switch back up and down once more. Time to go. Suddenly, there came a thunderous banging on the front door and a hollering to match it. 'Put that light out! Don't you know there's a war on?' Auntie Florrie rushed to the door to face an irate Air Raid Precaution (ARP) warden. They all turned to me – who else? 'You stupid girl – if there's a Jerry plane up there, he could be thinking you are signalling to drop a bomb. Mrs Fisher, check your blackout!' Off he went, huffing and puffing across the road, past the pig bin on the grass triangle opposite and into Ashmore Grove. Chastened, I put on my coat and collected my gas mask. My hand was firmly gripped and with a wavering, shaded torch, my mum navigated us back to East Ham. (It was good on the ferry, though.)

Not long after this my dad fell into the dock. Maybe he slipped, but Mum suggested he might have nipped one Johnnie Walker too many. Anyway, he arrived home resembling a large lump of flotsam and stinking to high heaven. His only regret was that his tobacco pouch was sodden. 'Easy done in the dark, Wol,' commiserated Mr Bosher the next day. Mum rolled her eyes skywards and curled her lip. Sympathy – forget it.

The air raids were becoming more frequent. Night-times were the worst. The German planes were flying fairly low up the Thames, targeting the docks, the ships and the factories. Sometimes it looked as if the whole of the river was on fire. There were gun emplacements in many of our London parks; most nights the firing seemed to be non-stop and we felt our ears would burst. The searchlights lit up the night sky and we watched as the German planes droned steadily on, dropping their bombs on London – unless the guns caught them and blew them up. Our planes chased, dived and fired in amongst them. Often it was a one-on-one dogfight and we held our breath waiting to see which plane, beaten, would scream to earth. Sometimes the

German planes were sent spiralling into one of the many barrage balloons that filled the sky and then, all tangled up, the plane would crash to the ground. The night-times were filled with frightening sounds: explosions, bells, the whooshing of bombs coming down, shouting and screaming. Most nights we crammed into Mr Bosher's shelter with his family and there we stayed until about five in the morning, or at least until the 'all clear' siren sounded. No one liked going down into the shelter – there were steep wooden steps, lots of bulging sandbags around, and down inside it smelt damp and clammy, but we felt safer down there than we did outside. Sometimes it wasn't just the Boshers and us. There were strangers too, if they were passing when the air-raid siren went. I hated it and always squashed up tight on Mum's lap. The worst part was when I wanted to go to the toilet. So many people to watch you; it was horrid. Down there we had a kettle and a teapot and the grown-ups would make tea; often the ladies did their knitting, but most of the time everyone sat silently and listened to the sound of the aircraft engines overhead, trying to work out which was which. Once our big guns started firing we couldn't hear ourselves speak. We waited in terror for the awful whoosh of a bomb coming down.

Farewell Priory

We left.
Upton Park deserters
That was us.
Our bubbles burst,
none of us wanted to go.
No more Rosie, no more larks.
Goodbye scooting in Central Park,
No up, down Priory on our bikes,
No more footy, no more fights.
I was sick on the 696.

Enough was enough. With bulging shopping bags, gas masks, identity cards and ration books, we three bundled on to a number 101 bus and began the journey to Auntie Florrie's, where we stayed until my dad found us a house to rent in Welling. We ended up in Hook Lane. There was a large corner garden, an apple tree and a massive hedge. Did I like it? No, I did not. Where were the people? Where were the other kids? It was so quiet. But bombs dropped on Welling too. My dad said the Germans were aiming for the Woolwich Arsenal, where hundreds of men and women were making munitions for our soldiers.

In our new home, we had a Morrison shelter, a large cage-like affair with mesh sides and a heavy steel top. It looked like a chicken run and was supposed to protect us from flying glass. Whenever the siren went, the side was unhooked and in we clambered. It wasn't comfortable, but at least it didn't smell like the Anderson and we didn't have to share it. I went through itchy chicken pox, mumps and measles in the Morrison, and suffered spoons of Virol, cod-liver oil and California Syrup of Figs. I had nowhere to run (except upstairs to the toilet)!

The wireless was very important. At the turn of a knob we got live music, cheerful voices and funny programmes. Tommy Handley and the cast of It's That Man Again (which we all called ITMA) were great favourites. They did so much to cheer people up when the days were so worrying and the nights so long.

Well, I suppose it couldn't last. I had to go to school, so down the road I went to Hook Lane Primary. The best part of the day was playtime, when I did handstands up against the shelter wall. The rest of it was pretty dull until one day, during an air raid, when the class was knitting covers for hot-water bottles, a teacher began to read us a story that transformed my life. I stopped knitting and hung on her every word. That evening I pestered my mum, demanding that she bought me the book. She didn't know what I was talking about, but I was desperate. Not that I didn't have other books. They filled up one corner of the Morrison shelter and, truth be told, I began to crawl into the shelter, air raid or not, to enjoy a read and escape into a silent world of my own.

Now it was all change: we were braving the bombs and learning to go without, but when Auntie Florrie told us they were having to move to Plymouth, we all cried. It seemed such a long way away. She said that Uncle Bert's boat was going to be based there and it was a very important dockyard. We didn't need to be told it was also very dangerous. Suddenly, Pam and Dennis were no longer just round the corner.

The air raids were now coming thick and fast, day and night. A bomb dropped near the top of Hook Lane and took away three-quarters of a house, leaving a bedroom open to the street, the bed just hanging on a few floorboards. The wallpaper had been pretty but there wasn't much of it left. Ambulances, ARP wardens and policemen were on the scene very quickly, but we weren't told how many people had been killed. About this time my mum took up smoking, so we had her Craven A as well as my dad's Nosegay tobacco on the dresser. The Germans were now bombing Plymouth dockyard and Plymouth town. I desperately longed to know what was happening to my cousins and my auntie and uncle.

Uncle Billy was working long hours in the Woolwich Arsenal and lodging in a house in Clifton Road, but we did see him from time to time. One evening he called in and gave us a bit of unexpected news. He was getting married – and oh, what excitement! He and his lady friend wanted me to be a bridesmaid! Mum worried about the clothing coupons but the outfit got made, so there I was in Dartford Registry Office in a long dress, looking like an overgrown raspberry, sporting white gloves and shoes with flowers in my hair, and having to behave nicely. I remember being surprised to see my dad in a smart suit, chatting away to a lot of strangers. Uncle Billy's new wife wore a silly hat that covered half her face and she did a lot of laughing. There were two children who came from somewhere and were meant to keep me company, but they didn't. Uncle Billy moved permanently into Falconwood Avenue and we waited politely to be invited.

We didn't dare try to visit Auntie Bessie: the journey was too long and we were fearful of getting caught in an air raid. They, of course, like us, spent long hours in a shelter. In fact, Bessie wrote to my mum that Uncle Albert was first in, or as she jokingly put it, 'Women and children first, after Albert!'

In January 1941, when I was seven, I had my last official birthday party. Our Christmas tree had always been left up until 11 January, when all the best crockery came out and was polished to perfection. There were no more kids from Priory, but Mum had rustled up two from down the road and she put on as best a spread as she could. She gave Betty and Georgie all the decorations off the tree. A lot of sparkle went their way. Amazingly, the siren didn't sound and when it was time for the tea party to end, we all huddled into our coats and stepped out into the cold winter night to take Betty and Georgie home.

So it went on. Would it ever end? We all did what we had always done, whenever we could. My dad went to work in what was left of the docks, my mum queued for rations and I went to school, spending more time in the shelter than in the classroom. I couldn't understand why I went; it just filled the day. We did a lot of colouring and singing, but I was much happier tucked up with my books in the Morrison shelter. Mum did times tables with me and taught me about kings and queens, and we read a lot together. Really, she was my best friend. I had a little storybook filled with pictures of a boy named Jesus and I was very attached to that.

One day I was kept home from school with a streaming cold. Mum had no alternative but to take me with her shopping. On the way back, with one precious egg and two oranges, she stopped outside a tall building with revolving doors and told me that this was the place where all my questions could be answered. It was the library; trouble was, I had to get a bit older before I could get a ticket. I went home nursing my soaring temperature and seemed to spend the night going round and round in those spinning doors, but next morning I remembered the library and knew it was the one place I wanted to be. Worn down by my aggravating perseverance, they finally let me in and there I spent the time between air raids, soaking up all I could lay my hands on. The ladies in the children's section were kind and patient. On one occasion, I spoke to a girl who went to Maryville Convent – the school in whose garden little Mary had stood, the one who had been close to Grandad on his special day.

The most desperately desired book in the world, according to me, turned up with that elusive teacher some long while later. I nervously asked her if she could read it again and write down the title. She did both and I was overjoyed. Transported to a beautiful, unknown and, most importantly, peaceful world, I didn't want her to stop, but the siren went. Clutching my precious bit of paper, I followed the others into the shelter. Next day, in the library, Miss Frost reached up to the shelf that housed the Gs and placed into my hands The Wind in the Willows. That book got me through the rest of the war and it has a never left me. I still search for Mole and Ratty along the riverbanks. They helped me to grow up; along with my devoted mum, they were my unfailing constants.

I am across the river now, and not quite as close to the Thames that had run through my early years, colouring and shaping the memories that will never leave me. Years of freedom and delight, years of fear and a multitude of kindly people, whose doors were never closed to me. These were the special, never-to-come-again years. How proud I am to have been born into a loyal working-class family and a vibrant, caring community. What a privilege to have been born an East Ender.

So life drifts on
and somewhere in the haze
the dear and steady Thames rolls by
past cranes, past docks
where chimneys pierce the London sky.
Grant in the light of memory
I'll hold it in my eye

Acknowledgements

My sincere thanks are given to the many encouraging people who have spurred this little book forward: my precious family and friends, the colleagues from the bookshop days, and Carrie Stay at Clockwork Moggy for her gentle illustrations. To our daughter Lisa, who originally broached the idea and who has been continually working on the project in so many ways. My apologies and a big hug to our daughter Victoria, who constantly wept for darling Nana Driscoll. My thanks and love beyond dimension to my dear husband Alan, whose support and patience are legendary. Of course, there would be no book if it wasn't for the expert professionalism of Lucy, Laura and Joe at Rethink Press; my thanks to them for their understanding and kindness from start to finish.

Author's Note

This book, mostly fact with a dash of fiction, tells of the times and lives of real people. The events were relayed to me as I was growing up. I am indebted to the superb Hulton publication *English Economic and Social History* by P.J. Larkin, against which I confirmed the historical facts.

To any unknown Terrys or Driscolls, I would like to say I am telling the story as I was told. Your version may vary; nevertheless, our strong families were phenomenal.

About the Author

Eileen Wiltcher attended Bexley Technical School for Girls, where she met inspiring English and drama teachers and fell in love with poetry. Having completed the expected commercial training, she held various secretarial positions in London, discovering (to her surprise) that the ability to make a good cup of tea was more important than her short-hand speed. What a waste of 120 words per minute!

At age nineteen she met her dear Alan. Soon after Piaggio introduced the Vespa Scooter, the newly-weds became members of the Vespa Club of Britain and chugged across Europe. Eileen was invited to write the page 'Mainly for Women' for a popular magazine called Scooter and Three-Wheeler. This was a busy and exciting time that culminated in the arrival of their first daughter, Lisa Marie. Busy before, hectic years now followed, especially with the birth of the couple's second daughter, Victoria, in 1969. Then the book trade called. Eileen and Alan opened their first bookshop in Eltham, South-East London. Collaborating with teachers and authors, Eileen spent many years running workshops, organising storytelling sessions and popular school bookshops. For Eileen, the best part was interacting with the children. 'You never knew when you had caught a spark and lit a candle.'

Eventually, retirement. What's that? Charity work, volunteering, a spell of reviewing books for the Children's Book Trust, proofreading for Afro London News, poetry club, more writing, and trying to keep up with four energetic grandsons keeps her busier than ever.

Priory Road Street Party celebrating the Coronation of King George VI & Queen Elizabeth, May 1937.
I am held by Mr Bosher, our neighbour. My dad is centre, with my grandad next to him and Uncle Billy far right.

Priory Road Street Party. Waiting for the photographer.
Mrs Smith, our neighbour, retrieving my hat.

East Ham Avondale Football Club 1902-1903.
My dad, Walter Levett, as a young man.

Uncle Billy's Wedding Day.
Uncle Billy on the left, my mum centre, my dad right and me as bridesmaid.

Me and Cousin Pam

Me, let loose on Southend Pier.

Auntie Florrie and Cousin Dennis
Such a saucy boy!

Auntie Bessie

Auntie Florrie

Me in the May Queen Parade.

Me in class photo, hating my ribbon!

From left to right.
Cousin Pam (baby), Auntie Florrie, Cousin Nessim, Auntie Bessie
and Cousin Esthriah

My mum, Beatrice Levett, taken in Dover.
A rare photo as she always shied away from the camera.

Lightning Source UK Ltd.
Milton Keynes UK
UKOW04f0039261117
313353UK00002B/15/P

9 781781 332726